WAYS WITH HAZEL AND HORN

by
BOB GRIFF JONES
and **MEURIG OWEN**

GWASG **Carreg Gwalch**

Foreword

My father started farming at Llangwm in 1947 and must have met Bob Griff soon after. My father, always an excellent judge of character eventually asked him to be his Bailiff at Hendre Garthmeilio. I was still at school when I first met him, but I remember a vast man (to me then) of tremendous strength, kindness and many jokes, a man who could do anything and everybody respected.

My father, a Director of Greenall Whitley's Brewery, brought home some long beer barrel staves which Bob Griff speedily transformed into pairs of skis for my brother and myself one snowy Christmas holiday. We had some dreadful falls brought about by insufficient snow and frozen molehills — how Bob laughed.

Later on when I married, Bob Griff made us a chair as a wedding present made of Welsh Oak, it has the family coat of arms on the back of it with rams heads on the arm rests. It is still a treasured possession in our hall and admired by all our many visitors.

Later still when my father retired, I took over the farming and worked with Bob. His abilities seemed to have no limits and I often wonder what his career would have been if he had gone to University and perhaps left Wales for other shores; I doubt whether he would have had a more successful life, if success is measured in those rare qualities of being respected by all, of creating some beautiful objects in wood and forming that bond with a succession of dogs to win many Sheepdog Trials.

I am sure the world should re-write its concept of success.

Michael Griffith
Greenfield, Trefnant

Contents

Chapter 1

'It's the old story about the cobblers shoes, isn't it!'

That's the way Bob Griff Jones jokes about his obsession with shepherds crooks. He remembers the sheepdog trials at Pistyll Rhaeadr in 1963 when he stood centre stage as a competitor (and won) and overheard a lady remarking: 'That can't be Bob Griff the stick maker, surely — with that great cudgel.'

'She was right to comment,' he says wrily, 'because I'd only that morning cut it out of a hedge on the way to the trials.'

His days as a successful trialist have long gone, but this arch stick maker is still without a crook to call his own!

He's lived in 'retirement' at Abergele these last twenty five years after a life in the Llangwm uplands, bringing with him his inborn stick making craft which he works at a bench in his garden shed.

His father — he'll tell you — was a country wood worker in the Uwchaled area around Cerrigydrudion, going from farm to farm with his tools in a bag on his back. A gate to be repaired, a cattle shed to be erected, even making a farm cart — he was the man to do the job.

But when still young his health broke down and even moving to Bryn Ffynnon, a small farm in Llangwm, expecting the change to effect an improvement, made little difference. The Multiple Sclerosis worsened and he became bed ridden for the last twenty eight years of his life. It was at his ailing father's bedside that Bob Griff aquired much of his expertise.

But there must have been a lot of woodworking talent in the blood already. Bob's brother — Gwil, Blaen Cwm, Cwmpenanner — now living in Ruthin was a dab hand with sticks.

And his grandfather, something of a country poacher, had this flair as well. Making his own mole traps out of wood.

And Bob as an eleven year old eagerly fetching and carrying. The old man, then in his eighties, would say: 'Young and old do well together, you know.' Bob, looking back, knows what he meant — quietly the old skills were being handed down.

Bob might have been a wood worker himself, following in the family tradition, had his father's health held good.

But he heard the call of the land — working on farms, eventually settling into a career as shepherd for the Griffiths family at Hendre Garthmeilo, Corwen, and staying there for twenty years. And meantime perfecting his art with sticks, enjoying the feel of wood and the craft of carving animal forms on the handles.

'Mind you, these weren't simply decorative things — they were a useful every day need for the country shepherd — for walking as well as coralling his flock.' So the shaft needs a comfortable handle which is also strong.

Bob Griff has his idol — W.R. Parry, Tyddyn Prior of Brynsiencyn, years ago, was the artisan king of stick making. They were easily as well crafted as

Leaning against the car at Pistyll Rhaeadr Sheepdog Trials with the godforsaken cudgel!

From left to right: Del (Marged Elin), my father William Jones, Annie, Mary, mother Jane Jones (with myself on her knee) and Jane. (Gwyneth and Gwilym weren't born then.)

Dafydd Roberts, Tyrpeg, Cefn Brith with a farm cart made by my father in the early twenties which was awarded first prize at Meirioneth County Show for a horse and cart turnout with full harness.

My mother and father at Brynffynnon, Llangwm with Aunty Maggie, Nilig from Cyffylliog.

the sermons of the ledgendary Rev. Dr John Williams from that same Anglesey village. The hall mark instantly recognised anywhere!

Bob's gift with wood became evident while still at school, etching out horses and dogs in timber.

And at the same time pursuing his interest in sheepdogs, later competing at local trials. And as his skill was perfected with better dogs, he realised the need for a good stick. 'So at eighteen years old, I had a go at it,' says Bob.

The convention before the war was for the all-wooden shepherds crooks — the idea of using horned handles was unknown — in Llangwm at any rate. 'But in the early fifties when I really applied myself, horns were gaining in popularity — with plenty available too.'

'Now it's a different story — what with polled rams being bred — finding a suitable horn is very difficult indeed.'

Now with his lifetime of stickmaking, there are a few hundred of the doyens art work about — and he remembers many hours of an evening spent happily at his workbench making them. He's retired now, and with the freedom to come and go as he pleases, Bob is in his element. And what is really surprising is that although he's suffered from Parkinsons these last six years, he's found a way to steady his hand when using the sharp chisels and

Grandfather and grandmother
(Thomas and Mary Jones) Ty'n Ffrith,
Llangwm, my father's parents.

7

the paintbrush. He gets his good days — but all in all he reckons that indulging his hobby gives his hands the beneficial theraputic excercises that they need.

'The number of hours you work at your craft is no measure of your professionalism,' Bob argues. 'There was a time when I first came to Abergele, having married Thelma, that I would make a business of my craft — carving wooden love spoons and so on, but — God help me — I'm a very poor salesman. And besides, I don't think you can successfully sell a stick by showing a sample of your work. For one thing no two sticks are the same, and certainly the horns for the handles are always different — and it's they which give the stick its character.'

Tools

Bob recalls the old time blacksmith from Maenan near Llanrwst — John Price Pont-y-Gath — saying that the craftsman's secret is to use as few tools as possible. With just a good fire, a hammer and chisel John could create farm implements of the highest quality. Before the war the Pont-y-Gath ploughs were very popular throughout Uwchaled and Penllyn.

They were the old fashioned kind which turned a furrow with a sharp upper edge. That meant that the corn thrown by the sower would fall down into the ridges to be nicely covered when the harrows were drawn over them.

The sight of seedling corn emerging in straight rows along where the ploughman had forged his straight and even furrow was a joy to be seen.

*'Five and seven and keep it straight' was the secret of ploughing in those days. And for the ploughing competitions a Pont-y-Gath plough was essential. 'You can bet your life that they would win the prizes!'

So as with the blacksmiths craft — stick making needs few tools: a bench, vice, various G clamps, drills (up to 9/16ths of an inch), hand saw, hack saw, a coping saw, a couple of small chisels, sand paper — both fine and coarse, a rasp and baling string!

For carving the horn you will need a small gouge and a V shaped chisel with a very sharp edge.

Bob Griff adds a salutory point. 'I'm convinced that everyone should learn how to sharpen their own tools, because that's part of the care you need in order to maintain them.'

'Years ago,' he reflects, 'you would hear the sharp edge of a scythe whistling through a hay or corn crop. It's the same with your hand tools — a good sharp edge adds pleasure to your work.'

And so he underlines an age old truth, 'Every true craftsman knows the value of a sharp cutting edge.'

'There's no sense at all in abusing your tools,' he adds.

* This referred to the furrow — five inches deep and seven inches wide.

HANDLE
(made out of horn)

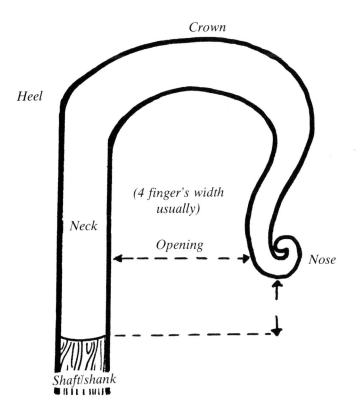

Crown

Heel

(4 finger's width usually)

Neck

Opening

Nose

Shaft/shank

Two traditional love spoons. The spoon on the left with its circular forms illustrates the lifecycle with the small spoons symbolising the idea of the loving couple united in wedlock.

The second spoon has two balls cradled in the handle, a symbol of the couple united in matrimony. The spoon at its end represents the idea of the young man being the provider of food for his bride: so by offering the spoon to his loved one he was making a promise to put food on the table during their married life. According to tradition the links in the chain represented the number of children with which the couple were to be blessed.

Some of the tools I have in my workshop. My favourite is the gouge — given to me years ago, during the second world war, by Dr Ifor Davies, Cerrigydrudion: there's not a single stick I've ever made that hasn't been touched by it!

Chapter 2

Different Kinds of Sticks

'Shepherds Crooks are what I normally make, but if the horn is not long enough it's quite easy to make a walking or market stick out of it.

The exact shape of the shepherding stick tends to vary with what the owner wants. But there is a marked difference between a market stick and a shepherds crook. The latter normally has the tip of the horn handle curled over — the old belief being that this would be where the shepherds would hang their lanterns. But it also has the more practical use these days of

 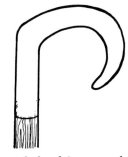 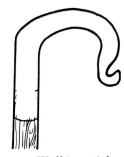

Shepherds stick.   *A stick for fair or market.*   *Walking stick.*

avoiding injury to the animal when catching a lamb or sheep, as well as channelling the neck into the cleft.

The present day shepherding sticks are longer. They usually measured to the owners hip bone and were handy then for catching lambs in springtime.

But with sheepdog trials becoming more popular there is demand for a longer stick to help in the final penning.

Another tendancy has been to make sticks purely for show purposes when the practical aspect is less important. So a stick with a long shaft was left that way in order to show it off better.

And speaking of long shafts, I suppose the longest that I have made have been Bishops Crooks, which have been over six foot long. But the problem with them is getting a sufficiently long horn for the handle, so that it matches the length of the shaft.

I solved the problem by making the handles out of wood. Elm I found ideal — and if a piece with a burr effect on it can be found this is good because then it is stronger and the mottled pattern is interesting.

Admittedly, strength in a Bishops Crook — used for ceremonials — is scarcely important, but its a point worth bearing in mind when doing ordinary sticks.

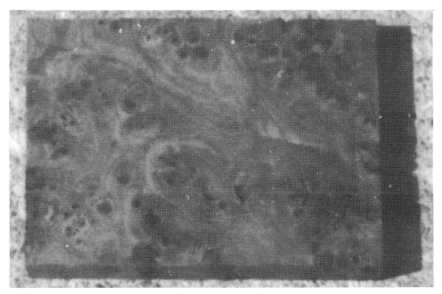

An example of burr (described in Welsh as 'Cat's Feet') a sort of cancer of the wood with small knots growing out of it, usually seen as knobbly outgrowth on oak and elm.

Wood

All you need for cutting the shafts is a small pruning saw and a pocket knife to trim off the side twigs. Plus a length of baling string to bundle them up. But be warned, freshly cut sticks can be very heavy!

The best are found in rough creeks where the land is poor, wet and rocky. They are much tougher than the long sticks that have grown rapidly on good land. Come to think of it, that applies to people too, doesn't it?

The other thing that I've observed is that you are more likely to find a fairly straight shaft growing in the middle of scrub. I say 'fairly straight' — intentionally — because however well they appear, they're rarely as straight as you'd expect, once they've been cut.'

Bob Griff — since his retirement — has had good friends scouting around for suitable material. 'My plastic hip replacements aren't up to allowing me to look for sticks on steep rocky slopes,' he says. 'Good as they are — it's ta-ta for me to do that.'

'There have been many that have helped over the years, but I must mention my old friend — now passed on — Wil, Dolwar Fach, Llanfyllin.

'He used to cut sticks for me, and for years my wife and I would go to meet him in Bala to pick them up, and we'd all have a feed of fish and chips before turning for home. He was a good old pal.'

Before the hip surgery Bob and his wife used to go to Lleuar Bach,

Cutting hazel wood with a pruning saw.

Pontllyfni. Thelma would stalk the wood, finding suitable sticks, while Bob followed with his pruning saw. But there was one unforgettable occasion when she stepped into a bog and sank up to her knees.

'When I reached her she'd somehow managed to get out of her wellingtons, and was standing on my best saw!'

'After a struggle I managed to rescue my saw — and the missus and her wellingtons,' says Bob.

'The best time to cut shafts is from early November to January when the sap is at its lowest. There's also the added advantage that in winter time the leaves will have fallen, making it much easier to find them.

The other reason for winter cutting is that the bark is firmer and will not shrivel as would be the case in summer time. This was very evident during 1994.

And here's a useful tip. Always select your shafts a lot thicker than you need to, because with having to let them dry out for a year before working on them, the shaft will become thinner.

Remember too, that you may get great losses from the woodworm getting into the wood during storage, so it's essential right from the start, to put protective oil on them. Some people believe it's best to lie the sticks horizontally in storage. But in my small garden shed its only possible to stand them up in a corner, and that seems to work all right.

Hazel

This by far the most popular wood for stick making. For one thing, you'll get various colours — mottled hazel for example, which grows on poor land giving you beautiful bark patterns. The red hazel you'll normally find on the better land.

If you're lucky you may find one where wild honeysuckle has entwined the stem, forming an interesting design. The longer the honeysuckle has been growing — say a couple of years — the deeper the impression.

I've even heard of people making an indentation with a knife around a hazel sapling similar to the honeysuckle mark, and leaving it there to grow on for a couple of years.

The problem then, is to remember which one it was! And even if you do remember its location, there is still the danger that someone else has been there and swiped it!

Blackthorn

This makes excellent sticks for walking, but you'll be very lucky to find a good one around here. I rely on a good friend who lives in Shropshire; but where he finds them, God only knows!

As I've said, they make first rate walking sticks, and the symmetric knots on the stem are attractive — but I find them too heavy for shepherds crooks.

Actually I make very few blackthorn sticks in the course of a year. It's one of the easiest to straighten out, but it also bends quicker than most.

The wood must dry out for at least a year before you can work on it.

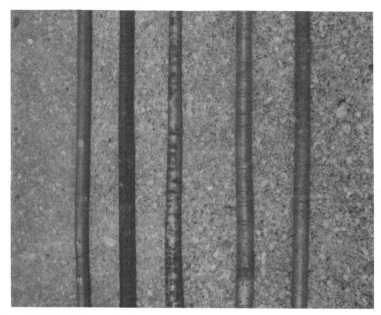

From left to right: ash, dark hazel, light hazel, cherry, mountain ash.

Ash
The ash too makes for a very tough stick — great for walking but the bark is a rather dull grey. With a bit of luck you might find an ash sapling that can be pulled up roots and all, so that you'll be able to make a stick with a wooden handle.

Holly
The bark of the holly looks a bit insipid, but even so, they make fine sticks. So it's best to de-bark them, leaving a white stick which is ideal for carving purposes. When taking the bark off it's usual to leave the knots reasonably prominent, so that you are left with quite a striking pattern. I once engraved the Lords Prayer along the stick's length to good effect.

Cherry Wood
The problem here is finding a suitable piece; that's just about the only reason that I've made so few of them in my time. Otherwise the bark is smooth and the pattern on the shaft is usually quite special.

Mountain Ash
Here again, this is quite suitable if you can manage to find one. They tend to grow in the uplands, but are regarded by many as being rather heavy. They were very useful in the old days as handles for farmyard racks and manure gaffs!'

17

A stick made of holly wood with the Lords Prayer engraved along its length.

A rams horn which has been sawn off too far from its base so that the nerve (quick) hole is not visible. Because of this you will lose up to a good two inches.

Chapter 3

Horns

'Any old horn won't do for the handle. For a start try to get a horn off a ram that's at least four years old, that usually means that it will be long enough; but with some it's possible that the nerve ends will have grown well into the horn. And again, for goodness sake try to avoid horns that have been heated and straightened when the rams were young. These will be hollow at the tips and have a blood clot in the horn.

Jacob and his flocks would be welcomed with open arms if they still roamed the land! But although they make beautiful crooks I'm afraid they're an almost endangered breed.

But having said that, here in Wales, luck is on our side, because the horn of the Welsh Mountain ram is the best we can get.

Take the Scotch Blackface for example, theirs are large heavy things in my opinion, and there's an awful lot of work rasping them down.

The same goes for the Swaledales — native sheep of the Pennines; they are big and twisting, and not as white as the Welsh horn. And it must be said the white pith is nearer the surface with these breeds too.

But horns are deceptive at best, and you can't be certain of their value until you have started working on them.

I've worked hard for hours before now rasping and cursing — sweating pots — only to find that the horn is hollow, or there's a nasty dark blemish in the pigment.

Some people are under the impression that you can make a handle out of any old horn — but you can't! The only other horn that I've used has been a buffalo's — a black horn. But they're not as good, and believe me no one wants to look at them if they can get a good rams horn.

Preparing the Horn

a. Cutting the Horn

In order to find out how far the nerve ends go into the horn, you should saw about two or three inches off the base; and remember, it's always best to take two cuts rather than sawing off too much at one go.

b. Softening the Horn

First of all, you'll need to boil the horn in water for about ten to fifteen minutes. Years ago, I used to boil them in oil, and that also worked perfectly — but doing it that way was a rather messy business.

Next place the horn in the vice between two metal plates (about 9x9 inches). Two pieces of hard wood can do almost as well — the only disadvantage being that wood takes longer to cool down. And it's really essential that the horn is properly cooled before taking it out of the vice, otherwise it's sure to return to its original shape.

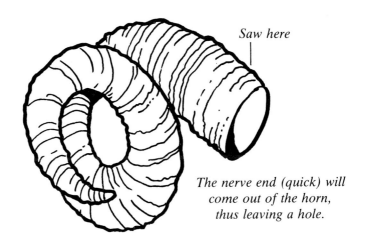

Saw here

The nerve end (quick) will come out of the horn, thus leaving a hole.

The vice or press.

c. Shaping the Handle.

Some horns are very strong, and often difficult to place in a vice at all. In such cases, it's a good idea to rasp the horn down a bit before boiling. You can also warm the horn a small section at a time with an electric paint stripper and then rasp it while it's still warm and soft. But don't overdo the heating because the scorch marks can sear deeply into the horn.

So gently does it, and plenty of patience!

Another important point as you work the horn is to watch that the pith doesn't come to the surface. It's presence is there, as in wood — but with the horn it appears as a thick line at its centre rather than circling under the outer shell.

The best way to tackle this is first to rasp the inner curve of the horn so that you don't reduce its size.

The two ways I've used regularly to shape the horn is either with a block or a length of cord.

You can, of course, use a combination of both — that is, get the horn into some semblance of shape with the cord, then finish off with the block.

It's only in the last couple of years that I've started using the block — a piece of wood about 1½ inches thick formed into the shape of a handle. It's a very handy way to do it.

Mind you, it's necessary to have block tenplates of different sizes because horns vary in sizes. The length of the horn of course, dictates the handle size, and that — in turn — the diameter of the shank.

Widening the horn is the most difficult by far. You do that by heating the

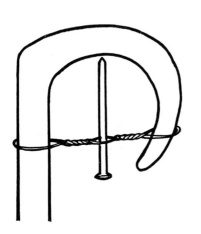

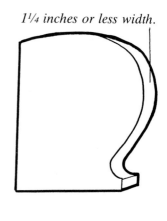

1¼ inches or less width.

outer curve, inch by inch, so that it flexes outwardly and stays in that shape after cooling down. I use a pick axe handle or something similar to lever it out as much as possible.

If it's a matter of closing up the handle, then the process is the same but this time the heat must be applied on the inside.

In both cases it's essential to have the horn in a vice — and in the case of closing the handle, take great care that the nail doesn't spring out at you!'

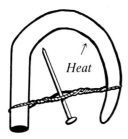

Baling cord tied across the horn. The nail at the centre when turned will tighten the cord and thus bend the horn.

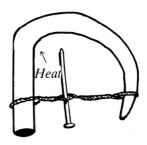

Heat up the horn at this point, and then turn the nail to pull it over.

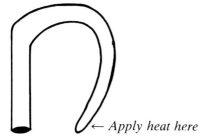

Heat up a little here in order to turn the point outwards.

A stick which has kicked up too much as you might say — that is, the handle is rising too much.

A stick without enough kick — with the hande less than square with the shank.

Chapter 4

Preparing the Shaft

'Given a year or more to dry out — the shank will be ready to place in the horn. First you should cut off the side shoots and pare back the knots so that they're reasonably smooth on the shaft. Then I apply fine sandpaper on the rougher parts, taking care not to rub too hard for fear of spoiling the natural pattern — and its also so easy to take the bark off and then you're left with a white stick!

'Tis said that 'A straight stick will hold up the world.' And that's almost true! A stick with a bow in it gives way much sooner than a straight one.

And as the old Welsh song goes about granny's walking stick, the shape of the handle is important to direct the weight straight down the shaft. So proportion and symmetry is important as we create the stick.

If the shaft needs to be straightened then the first thing to do is to apply heat to the relevant part then bend the shaft well over — rather more than you need to, because it's sure to whip back a bit. Then continue the process for the entire length until the shaft is straightened. A vice with a fairly smooth jaw is useful for doing this, but take care not to damage the bark. A piece of leather or plastic protection over the part that's in the vice will provide a useful safeguard.

Matching the Shaft to the Crook

So when you have the horn smoothly shaped and ready it is time to think of drilling a hole for the shaft to fit into it. Here, the heel — so to speak — is the most important part of the crook. So in order to match the heel so that it lies true, I use an iron pipe of 1 to 1½ inch in diameter which has been cut down the middle to act as a collar over the two sections in a vice.

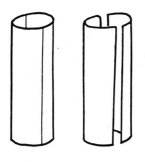

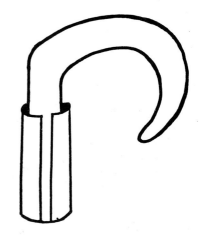

A piece of iron pipe about 1" - 1½" in diameter which has been sawn down the middle.

24

As the horn is squeezed, the untidy hole in the horn base which once contained the pith will go smaller, and then it's necessary to clean up the hole with a drill.

When I started stick making — umpteen years ago now! — I always used the method described in diagram 1.

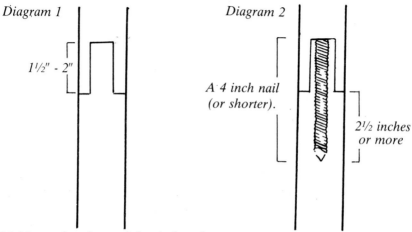

Diagram 1

1½" - 2"

Diagram 2

A 4 inch nail (or shorter).

2½ inches or more

Making a dowel out of the shaft and a ⁹/₁₆th inch hole in the horn.

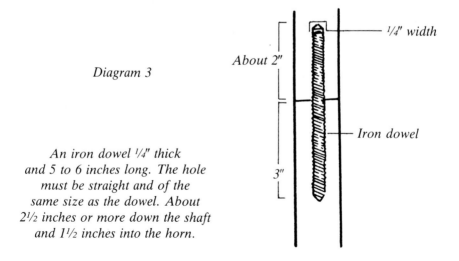

Diagram 3

About 2"

¼" width

Iron dowel

3"

An iron dowel ¼" thick and 5 to 6 inches long. The hole must be straight and of the same size as the dowel. About 2½ inches or more down the shaft and 1½ inches into the horn.

But as time went on, ideas changed — even in stick making there are fashions and phases! And that's when it became usual practice to follow the diagram 3 method — that is putting a ¼ inch iron insert to join up the crook to the shaft.

This was a far easier way and allowed for greater flexibility; if necessary you could even bend the insert to give a straight finish. So I began doing it this way too. But as time went on I was getting messages from the lads — and women, who were using them with their flocks that the sticks tended to split.

Not by giving the dogs a beating — heaven forbid, they'd never do that! It happened when they came to the penning and the need to strike the ground when sometimes the sheep went in a flurry in the wrong direction or the odd stupid ewe refused to co-operate.

So by beating the ground some of the sticks would split down from below the handle — and that meant a new shaft had to be fitted.

So there was nothing for it — I had to go back to plan 1. And believe you me — the flow of returned split sticks slowed down dramatically. That proved to me at any rate, that there was a flaw with the iron insert method (it was either that, or the handlers weren't beating the ground so hard — and I don't think that was the case somehow!)

Then came the idea of putting a 3 to 4 inch nail down through the centre of the wooden insert (see diagram 2). The nail head, of course has to be sawn off, and a hole drilled so that the wood doesn't split. And remember not to put glue in with the nail or else you won't be able to remove it — if you need to.

At Bryntrillyn sheepdog trials in the 1980's.

26

The hole I end up with is usually 9/16 of an inch, so in order that the bore into the hole is accurate, I start off with ¼ or ⅛ inch bit. If that hole isn't true, then you still have a chance to square it up with the larger drill. I always think it's good to have that second opportunity; meanwhile taking time to size it up — and to give it a quiet lecture with a few choice words for good measure!!

I use an electric drill for the smaller holes and for the 9/16 inch; the ½ inch is fairly strong when the nail is down the middle of the wooden insert. After boring the hole in the crook, you'll need to select a shaft which will match up to it, bearing in mind that this needs to be slightly slimmer than the horn where they meet up.

Then you need to rasp the horn down to the diameter of the shaft taking care that you don't damage the bark. So it's a fine rasp, sand paper, a steady eye — and away you go: working with the grain of the horn using the fine sandpaper for the final smooth finish.

Now to the wooden insert — the most important part of all. This needs to fit in tightly, so that there's no slack when it's finally in place. Any movement when they're joined together is of no use: that would mean doing another

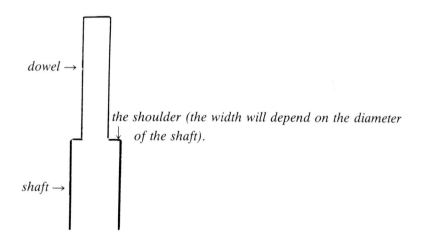

dowel →

the shoulder (the width will depend on the diameter of the shaft).

shaft →

The shoulder here must be perfectly square and clean.

27

dowel, possibly further down the same stick — if that is still long enough.

If the horn and the stick shoulder do not meet up together satisfactorily you should put a pencil mark on the shank (in order to put it back as before) then make a shallow saw cut around the shank, then take them apart, clean up and try again. Remembering to fit the stick in exactly as before. Repeat the procedure until you have it absolutely right.

Before finally putting it all together, make sure that the horn is clean before putting glue on the wooden dowel and inside the horn for pressing them home. If this has been done correctly you will have it all as one unit, firm and without any unseemly cracks.

Now you'll need to keep it tightly together while the glue sets firmly. Personally I use baling twine for this — over the handle and down to the tip of the stick, and twisting it so tightly that you can almost play a tune on it!

The horn ready to be put on the shaft.

As a rule, I clean up and carve images on the crook — where that is needed — before putting them together for the last time. I know from experience that it's much easier to do the art work **before** the horn goes on the shaft.

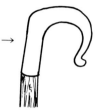

The handle that leans forward (to the right) is totally unacceptable.

If the handle leans back — to the left — then that's almost as good as having it totally upright. Often a carpenter will make a gate out of true with the near upright higher — knowing that with use it will drop down naturally.

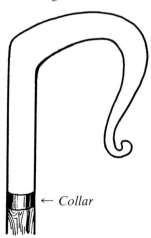

← *Collar*

As a rule I never place a collar on a stick. That is, the thin horn circle covering the join. When I see that, it immediately occurs to me to ask: is it there to strengthen the stick or to cover up mistakes?

There's no doubt that a collar prevents the wood from splitting when using a metal insert. But where the insert is of wood and the horn fits well I see no reason for a strengthener.

   And after all if the job is well done — it's a poor craftsman who wants to hide his handywork.'

Capturing an old farmyard scene in wood — before it gets all mechanical!

Chapter 5

Carving

Seeing Tecwyn Pen Gob working his dogs over at Gellioedd — trained for action like a team of cart horses: drawing a sack — a dog to each corner — delighted Bob Griff.

He thrills to the memory. For him a fine working sheepdog is the highest form of art as is the skill and patience of the trainer.

So there's no wonder that as a young lad caught up in awe mid the sights of graceful animals on an upland farm — the dogs, the sheep and rams and the shire horses — he would sketch them with a pencil. Hundreds of them.

At fifteen even carving — etching their outline in wood. And competing at local eisteddfodau, rising to the craftwork challenge and pitting his skill. He owes a lot to that — honing his artistic ability.

He was carving and drawing before ever getting caught by the sticks and crooks!

He still uses the techniques learnt in childhood. The drawing comes first — on paper or well planed wood.

'Maybe I am lucky that I'm sometimes able to draw quite well,' he'll say in his modest way.

'Tracing is an option — but that only gives the outline: doesn't show the sparkle in the eyes, the sensitivity of the ears and the glisten of muscle in the

This plaque which I made for the engraving competition in the National Eisteddfod at Machynlleth in 1981 was awarded first prize. The design was by E. Meirion Roberts, Old Colwyn.

The Last Supper (Leonardo da Vinci): a work which I carried out in oak for the 150th anniversary of Bethabara Baptist Chapel at Llangernyw in 1980.

The Cledwyn Roberts Memorial Trophy (Llangernyw). The design was by Gerallt Lloyd Owen, and I worked the carving. It is awarded (to be held for a year) for the best lyric/poem in the popular radio series on Radio Cymru, Talwrn y Beirdd.

33

creeping leg movement.'

And so the sketching and carving led to commissions. A memorial plaque for Wales' eminent men of culture: R. Williams Parry the poet, Llwyd o'r Bryn the countryman from Sarnau — both appreciators of the skill of words and repartee. Planned by Ifor Owen and carved by Bob Griff.

Even carving trophies to the design of National Eisteddfod artist Meirion Roberts, Old Colwyn, for the popular Ymryson y Beirdd competition on Welsh Radio — the Rolant o Fôn Commemorative Award.

Bob's been through a hard drill. 'You learn a lot by working with people like that,' he'll say. 'Reacting to the challenge of ever higher standards.'

So tip number one is to practice your carving on wood first of all before moving on to working with horn. Horn isn't so easy — the surface area is smaller and it's always difficult working on a curved smooth surface.

And besides, the horn itself is much harder and there's always the danger of chiseling too deeply if you're not careful.

Having penciled your drawing of a dog on the horn, comes the work with the small V chisel, lightly tracing the outline followed with the small gouge.

Bob warns: 'The secret is not to chisel too deeply — just tiny cuts at a time until you'll see the shape emerging.'

I carved out this miniature bardic chair for 'Cyfarfod Bach' Gellioedd in the sixties. (A local eisteddfodic event) in Llangwm.

This is a plaque I carved as a trophy for the sheepdog trials held at Brynffynnon, Llangwm some time ago. This scene — a ram confronting a sheepdog — is one I often depict on a horn handle.

Now you need to make sure that the surfaces are smoothed — a chisel with a lesser curve in it will take away the unecessary marks. The final flourish is with an ordinary narrow, but very sharp, chisel — highlighting the legs and head of the dog.

'Ideally get a proper dog, and study it very carefully to make sure that you have got the head angle, the eyes and ears, and of course the tail, right,' says

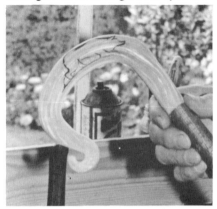

Outline of a dog on the horn.

The finished work.

A stick that's gone to America to a young lady called Hope. I was asked to carve out her name in Welsh on the handle.

Bob.

So next comes the colouring: water paint for the stick, Indian ink for the black and emulsion for the white parts.

But Bob issues a reminder: 'The dogs are never consistently black, nor the white pure, so bring a natural shading into the paintwork. Some highlights, of course, and then a darker hue around the feet.'

So some general points to bear in mind.

First try out your carving in wood — and always aim for something bigger than you intended.

If possible, take a long careful look at the animal you're portraying. It's often difficult to position the eyes correctly on each side of the head; and again the horn will present its own challenge in this respect.

Now a few points coming to the final detail.

Use the fine rasp and sandpaper with utmost care, because you can so easily obliterate your entire work by rubbing too hard. And always remember to work the sandpaper with the grain of the horn. Your aim is to get a smooth finish which will look well when the varnish has been applied.

Polish versus varnish!
Polish is often used for competition purposes.

But Bob begs to differ. 'I normally use varnish,' he says, 'because for one thing it's not easy to polish a handle that's been painted, and furthermore varnish stands up to the weather better than polish — and that's important because most of my sticks go to shepherds who work the hills in all climates.'

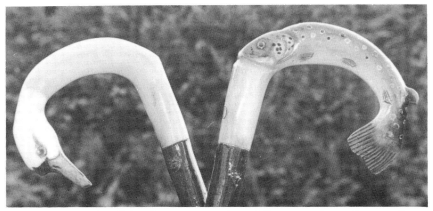

There's not much call for these two creations. They appeal mostly to walkers and fishermen — as a walking stick, of course!

On the left: a portrait of old Jess, Aled Owen, Penyfed, Llangwm's bitch,
which I was able to carve out on a plain handle after the stick had taken top
prize at the Machynlleth National Eisteddfod. It's quite often the case that
shepherds want their own favourite dogs portrayed on the handle.
I've carved many handles with the owners name on them — like the one on the
right. Another favourite request is for a rams head on the heel. With this
particular stick I also added a leek on the crown — for good measure!

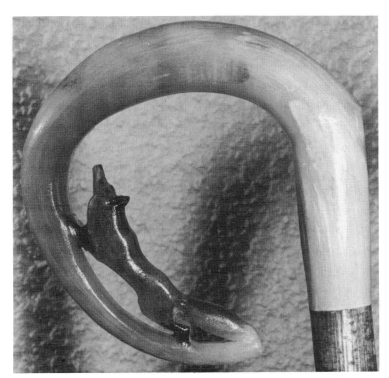

This unusual design calls for skilfull detailed carving. The fox — so far — is the only animal that I've ever carved on the inside of the handle.

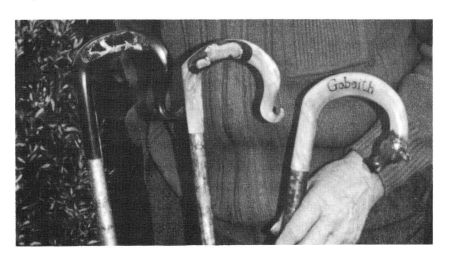

Chapter 6

Now to the contentious question about the length, diameter and weight of a shepherds crook.

Bob reckons that the Scottish and Northern England shepherds use much heavier and longer sticks than we do in Wales.

But which is right? Bob reasons like this: 'The horns of the Scotch Blackface and Swaledales are cumbersome and large in comparison to the Welsh. And the pith is nearer the surface, so it follows that the horns are left large, and the shafts need to be big and heavy to match.'

So its everyone to his fancy. But with the smaller Welsh horns the sticks need to be smaller and lighter to go with them.

'In any case,' says Bob, 'what's the point in having an unwieldy shepherding stick to attend to the smaller Welsh Mountain sheep anyway?'

'When I was a shepherd in the hills the crook was used to catch the spring lambs for cleaning up. So the larger the stick — the more awkward it was to use.'

And what about the apperture of the crook? This can vary with where you are farming. 'Some of those big sheep on the lowlands have necks like bacon pigs,' says Bob Griff, 'whereas the Welsh Mountain sheep have quite a small neck.'

But there's hardly the need for a shepherds crook with those big breeds. 'To tell you the honest truth, those mules — the cross bred sheep — are so large, you need hardly bend to catch one.'

'So I suppose it's possible to go to extremes when making a stick. Shafts straight as a shot and handles without blemish, — polished and shaped so that you scarcely ever believe that it was once a rams horn.'

So for the novice stick maker the task appears impossible. 'For my part I take the view that encouragement is better than criticisim,' says Bob.

That's something that he learnt at his fireside at Bryn Ffynnon years ago. A neighbour called, and said to his Mam, 'I could sing quite well Jennie — until that Boba Ffrith Gwair told me to stop making a din in his old choir!'

'She never sang a note after that,' says Bob, 'now there's a lesson there somewhere, isn't there!'

The secret is to look and listen — and help will come from the most unlikely places. That's Bob's philosophy.

'There's none so blind as those who don't want to see,' and it's a poor lookout if you can't see something worthwhile in the efforts of your fellow human beings.

Bob offers comforting thoughts to the newcomer. Even for him there are days when nothing goes right. A series of duff horns — one damn thing after another! — then maybe the silver lining, and your luck changes.

'One thing is certain,' says Bob, 'you need old Job's patience. And sometimes it helps to talk to yourself — or to the stick! And thank goodness they both have the good grace not to answer you back!'

They can be bought from various places — on stands at the larger sheepdog trials or by mail order.

'I used to make my own years ago,' says Bob Griff, 'By sawing an inch off the end of a copper pipe (½ inch diameter) and squeeze it on to the end of the stick. Then a couple of dents knocked in around its edge so that it gripped on to the stick.'

But for competition purposes it's customary to make one out of horn. First you shape the end of the stick to take the ferule, then drill into a piece of horn to the correct size and dress it tidily so that it's ready to be put in place.

'And there you are, the stick complete.'

'We live and learn — and I reckon I'm still learning newer and easier ways of doing the things I enjoy.'

One further step remains — fixing the ferule at the end of the stick.

Usually of metal or rubber.

'There's an old Welsh saying which is appropriate for me: 'If you're not strong — be crafty!' And that's my aim, to do the things I used to do when young — but better!'

'I remember the Rev. J.C. Jones, Dinas Mawddwy preaching in Gellioedd Chapel years ago: 'I'm eighty,' said he, 'and I haven't preached my best sermon yet!'

'And neither have I' said Bob.

First published in Welsh
© Bob Griff 1995
Adapted by Meurig Owen

English text © 1996

ISBN: 0-86381-367-4

Cover illustration
and some black & white photographs:
Sion Jones, Abergele;
Drawings: Anne Lloyd Morris

First published in 1996 by Gwasg Carreg Gwalch,
Iard yr Orsaf, Llanrwst, Gwynedd, Wales.
☎ (01492) 642031

Printed and published in Wales.